PUBLIC SCHOOL LAW OF NORTH CAROLINA

ISSUED IN PURSUANCE OF LAW
BY THE SUPERINTENDENT OF PUBLIC INSTRUCTION

RALEIGH
EDWARDS & BROUGHTON, AND E. M. UZZELL, STATE PRINTERS
PRESSES OF EDWARDS & BROUGHTON
1901

PREFACE.

This pamphlet is issued in accordance with section 7 of the School Law. Some changes have been made in the School Law with a view to simplify its construction and application to schools, such as experience and careful observation suggests.

Upon oneness of purpose and prompt efficient execution of the law depends the success of our public schools. I earnestly beg the hearty cooperation of every school officer and the friends of education in the State, to the end that public education may prosper and the demands of the day be met. While there is abundant opportunity to exercise wise discretion given to the different school officers, I trust that this fact will not destroy harmony of action by captious independence or unmeaning variety. We must strive in concert for the interest of schools, if progress is made.

Added to the School Law is an act ratified March 11, 1901, correcting some typographical errors which is commended for perusal. The State Text-Book Law is also appended.

T. F. TOON,
Superintendent Public Instruction.
Raleigh, N. C., May 1, 1901.

PUBLIC SCHOOL LAW

OF

NORTH CAROLINA.

SECTION 1. The State Board of Education shall, on the first Monday in August of each and every year, apportion among the several counties of the State all the school funds which may be then in the treasury of the said board, and order a warrant for the full apportionment to each county, which said apportionment shall be made on the basis of the school population, but no part of the permanent school fund shall be apportioned or distributed, but only the income therefrom. The State Auditor shall keep a separate and distinct account of the public school funds, and of the income and interest thereof, and also of such moneys as may be raised by State, county, and capitation tax, or otherwise, for school purposes. *State Board of Education to apportion school funds. Apportionment made on basis of school population. Only income of permanent fund applied. Separate accounts of funds to be kept.*

SEC. 2. Upon the receipt of the requisition of the Treasurer of any county, duly approved by the chairman and secretary of the County Board of Education for the school fund which may have been apportioned to said county, the State Board of Education shall issue its warrants on the State Auditor for the sum due said county whereupon the said Auditor shall draw his warrant on the treasurer of the State Board of Education in favor of such County Treasurer for the amount set forth in the warrant of the said State Board. *On requisition County Treasurer properly approved, State Board of Education to issue warrant on Auditor and Auditor on Treasurer for amount apportioned to said county.*

SEC. 3. The State Treasurer shall receive and hold as a special deposit all school funds paid into the treasury, and pay them out only on the warrant of the State Auditor, issued on the order of the State Board of Education in *School funds paid into treasury, how held and paid out.*

What constitutes valid voucher in hands of State Treasurer for school funds. favor of a County Treasurer, duly endorsed by the County Treasurer in whose favor it is drawn, and it shall be the only valid voucher in the hands of the State Treasurer for the disbursement of school funds.

Proceeds of lands granted by U. S. to N. C., moneys stocks, bonds and property belonging to educational fund. SEC. 4. The proceeds of all lands that have been or may hereafter be granted by the United States to this State, and not otherwise appropriated by this State or the United States, also all moneys, stocks, bonds and any other property now belonging to any State fund, for the purposes of education, also the net proceeds of sales of swamp lands belonging to the State, and all other grants, gifts or devises that have been made or hereafter may be made to this State, and not otherwise appropriated by this State or by the terms of the grant, gift or devise, shall be paid into the State Treasury, and, together with so much of the ordinary revenue of the State as may be set apart for that purpose, shall be faithfully appropriated for establishing and maintaining a system of free public schools, as established in pursuance of the Constitution.

Property belonging to county school fund, proceeds from sale of estrays, penalties, forfeitures, fines, fines for breach of military laws, moneys paid for military exemption, and taxes for liquor license and auctioneers appropriated in each county for public schools. SEC. 5. All moneys, stocks, bonds and other property belonging to a county school fund, also the net proceeds from sales of estrays, also the clear proceeds of all penalties and forfeitures, and of all fines collected in the several counties for any breach of the penal or military laws of the State, and all moneys which shall be paid by persons as equivalent for exemption from military duties; also the net proceeds of any tax imposed on licenses to retailers of wines, cordials, or spirituous liquors and to auctioneers, shall belong to and remain in the several counties, and shall be faithfully appropriated for establishing and maintaining free public schools in several counties as established in pursuance of the Constitution. The amount

Annual report to Superintendent of Public Instruction. collected in each county shall be reported annually to the State Superintendent of Public Instruction. The Solicitors of the several judicial districts, criminal and inferior courts, shall prosecute all penalties, and forfeited recognizances entered in their courts respectively, and as compensation for their services shall receive a sum to be fixed by the Court, not more than five per centum of the amount collected upon such penalty or forfeited recognizance for the collection of which execution was found to be necessary. *(Duties of solicitors as to the penalties and forfeited recognisances. Compensation.)*

SEC. 6. If the tax levied for the State for the support of the public schools shall be insufficient to maintain one or more schools in each school district for the period of four months, then the Board of Commissioners of each county shall levy annually a special tax to supply the deficiency for the support and maintenance of said schools for the said period of four months or more. The said tax shall be collected by the Sheriff in money, and he shall be subject to the same liabilities for the collection and accounting of said tax as for other taxes. The said tax shall be levied on all property, credits and polls of the county; and in the assessment of the amount on each the Commissioners shall observe the constitutional equation of taxation; and the funds thus raised shall be expended in the county in which it is collected, in such manner as the County Board of Education may determine for maintaining the public schools for four months at least in each year. But the County Board of Education shall not be required to expend upon a district containing less than sixty-five pupils the same sum it may give to larger districts, notwithstanding an inequality of length of school terms may be the result. The County Board of Education, on or before the annual meeting of the Commissioners and Justices of the Peace for levying county taxes, shall make an estimate of the amount of money necessary to maintain the schools for four months and submit it to the County Commissioners. *(Levy of special tax to maintain four months' schools in each district provided for. Tax, how collected. On what levied. Funds, how and where expended. County Board of Education to estimate amount necessary to maintain four months' schools.)*

SEC. 7. The Superintendent of Public Instruction shall have the school laws published in pamphlet form and distributed on or before the first day of May of each year. He shall send to each officer a circular letter, enumerating his duties as prescribed in this act. He shall have printed all the forms necessary and proper for the purposes of this chapter, and shall look after the school interest of the State, and report biennially to the Governor, at least five days previous to each regular session of the General Assembly, which report shall give information and statistics of the public schools and recommend such improvements in the school law as may occur to him. He shall keep his office at the seat of government, and shall sign all requisitions on the Auditor for the payment of money out of the State Treasury for school purposes. Copies of his acts and decisions, and of all papers kept in his office and authenticated by his signature and official seal, shall be of the same force and validity as the original. He shall be furnished with such room, fuel and stationery as shall be necessary for the efficient discharge of the duties of his office.

SEC. 8. The Superintendent of Public Instruction shall direct the operations of the system of public schools and enforce the laws and regulations in relation thereto. It shall be his duty to correspond with leading educators in other States, and to investigate systems of public schools established in other States, and, as far as practicable, render the results of educational efforts and experiences available for the information and aid of the Legislature and State Board of Education.

SEC. 9. It shall be the duty of the Superintendent of Public Instruction to acquaint himself with the peculiar educational wants of the several sections of the State, and he shall take all proper means to supply said wants, by counseling with County Boards of Education and County

Superintendents, by lectures before Teachers' Institutes, and by addresses to public assemblies on subjects relating to public schools and public school work, and he shall be allowed for traveling expenses and for additional clerical assistance five hundred dollars per annum. *Allowance for traveling expenses and additional clerical assistance.*

SEC. 10. In case the State Superintendent shall have sufficient evidence at any time that any County Superintendent of Schools or any member of the County Board of Education, is not capable of discharging or is not discharging the duties of his office as required by this act, or is guilty of immoral or disreputable conduct, he shall report the matter to the County Board of Education, which shall hear evidence in the case, and if, after careful investigation they shall find sufficient cause for his removal, they shall declare the office vacant at once and proceed to elect his successor. Either party may appeal from the decision of the County Board of Education to the State Board of Education, which shall have full power to investigate and review the decision of the County Board of Education. This section shall not be construed to deprive each County Superintendent of the right to try his title to said office in the courts of the State. *Proceedings for removal of County Superintendent of Schools and election of successor. Appeal. County Superintendent may try title to office in State courts.*

SEC. 11. The State Superintendent of Public Instruction is authorized to employ a clerk at a salary of one thousand dollars per annum and a stenographer at a salary of two hundred and fifty dollars per annum to be paid monthly by the State Treasurer on the warrant of the Auditor, out of any funds which may be in the Treasury not otherwise appropriated. *Superintendent of Public Instruction authorized to employ clerk and stenographer. Salaries.*

SEC. 12. The General Assembly shall appoint three men in each county of good business qualifications and known to be in favor of public education, who shall constitute a County Board of Education, which board shall enter upon the duties of its office immediately upon the qualification of a majority of its members. In case of vacancy by *County Board of Education, how appointed. When to enter upon duties.*

death, resignation or otherwise, said vacancy shall be filled by the other members of the County Board of Education. Members of the County Board of Education herein provided for shall hold office until the first Monday in July, 1903, at which time the Board of County Commissioners in each county shall elect the Board of Education and every two years thereafter.

SEC. 13. The County Board of Education shall be a body corporate by the name and style of "The County Board of Education of .... County," and by that name shall be capable of purchasing and holding real and personal estate, of building and repairing school-houses, of selling and transferring the same for school purposes and of prosecuting and defending suits for or against the corporation. They shall have power and authority and it shall be their duty to institute and prosecute any and all actions, suits, or proceedings against any and all officers, persons, or corporations or their sureties for the recovery, preservation, and application of all moneys or property which may be due to or should be applied to the support and maintenance of the school except in case of breach of bond on the part of the Treasurer of the County School Fund, in which case action shall be brought by the County Commissioners as provided in section forty-seven. The County Board of Education and all other school officials in the several counties shall obey the instructions of the State Superintendent and accept his constructions of the school law. The time of opening and closing the public schools in the several public school districts of the State shall be fixed and determined by the County Board of Education in their respective counties, and the Board of Education shall have power and authority to fix and determine the methods of conducting the public schools in their respective counties, so as to furnish the most advantageous methods of education available to the children attending the public schools in the several counties of the State, and the County Board of Education and the County Superintendent of Schools shall have full power to make all just and needful rules and regulations governing the conduct of teachers and pupils as to attendance on the schools, discipline, tardiness, and the general government of the schools. Rules and regulations governing schools.

NOTE.—No pupil shall be allowed to attend any school while any member of the household is sick of small-pox, diphtheria, measles, scarlet fever, yellow fever, typhus fever, or cholera, or within two weeks after the death, recovery, or removal of such sick person. Any pupil coming from such household shall bring proper certificate from attending physician, or health officer. Committeemen and teachers failing to enforce this are subject to indictment. Laws 1893, ch. 214, page 13.

SEC. 14. In addition to all other duties and powers imposed and conferred upon them by law, the County Board of Education shall have general control and supervision of all matters pertaining to the public schools in their respective counties and are given the powers to execute, and are charged with the due execution of the school laws in their respective counties, and all powers and duties conferred and imposed by this act, or the general laws of the State respecting public schools which are not expressly conferred and imposed upon some other official, are conferred and imposed upon said County Board of Education; and an appeal shall lie from all other county school officers to said board. Additional powers of County Boards of Education.

SEC. 15. The County Board of Education shall have power to investigate and pass upon the moral character of any teacher in the public schools of the county, and to dismiss such teacher, if found of bad moral character, also to investigate and pass upon the moral character of any applicant for a teacher's certificate or for employment as teacher in any public school in the county, such investiga- Powers of County Boards over public school teachers and applicants.

tion shall be made after written notice, of not less than ten days, to the person whose character is to be investigated. The said board shall have power to issue subpœnas for the attendance for witnesses, a disobedience to which subpœnas shall, without legal excuse, be a misdemeanor punishable by a fine of not more than fifty dollars or imprisonment for not more than ten days. Subpœnas may be issued in any and all matters which may lawfully come within the powers of said board, and which in the discretion of the board should be investigated. And it shall be the duty of the Sheriffs, Coroners and Constables to serve such subpœnas upon payment of their lawful fees for service of subpœnas issued from the Superior Court of the State. Appeals provided for in this act shall be regulated by rules to be adopted by the board. The Superior Courts of the State may review any action of the County Board of Education affecting any one's character or right to teach.

SEC. 16. The County Board of Education on the second Monday in July, 1901, and biennially thereafter, shall elect a County Superintendent of Schools, who shall be at the time of his election, a practical teacher or who shall have had at least two years experience in teaching school and who also shall be a man of liberal education and shall otherwise be qualified to discharge the duties of his office as required by law due regard being given to experience in teaching. Said Superintendent must be of good moral character and shall hold his office for a term of two years from the date of his election and until his successor is elected and qualified. Immediately after the election of the County Superintendent of Schools the chairman of the County Board of Education shall report to the State Superintendent of Public Instruction the name, address, experience, and qualifications, of the person elected, and the person elected shall report to the State Superintendent as soon as he shall have qualified, the date of such qualification. In case of vacancy by death, resignation, or otherwise, the County Board of Education shall fill said vacancy. The members of the County Board of Education and County Superintendent of Schools have the authority to administer oaths to teachers and all subordinate school officials where an oath is required of the same: *Provided,* that any person who has filled the office of County Superintendent for four years next preceding the passage of this act shall be eligible to such office in Bertie and Bladen Counties, if the election of such person meets the approval of the State Board of Education.

Person elected to report date of qualification. Vacancy, how filled.

Power to administer oaths.

Proviso as to Bertie and Bladen Counties.

NOTE.—The powers of the County Board of Education have been enlarged, their duties increased, and consequently their responsibility is greater. The schools will be what you and a Superintendent of your own selection makes them. A wise execution of the law by a wide-awake board and an energetic Superintendent will insure progress in public schools.

SEC. 17. The County Board of Education of each county shall on the second Monday in July, 1901, and biennially thereafter, appoint in each of the townships of the county three intelligent men of good business qualification, who are known to be in favor of public education, who shall serve for two years from the date of their appointment as School Committeemen in their respective townships and until their successors are elected and qualified. If a vacancy shall occur at any time by death, resignation or otherwise it shall be the duty of the County Board of Education to fill such vacancy. The County Board of Education shall have the power to pay out of the reserve school fund to each member of the Township Committee thus appointed one dollar per day for not more than four days per annum. On the second Monday in July, nineteen hundred and one, and biennially thereafter, the County Board of Education in each county may, if they deem best, instead of electing Township Committee-

Appointment of Township School Committeemen.

Qualifications.

Term of office.

Vacancy, how filled.

Compensation.

County Board of Education may elect three Committeemen for each school.

men, elect for each school of the several townships three School Committeemen of intelligence and good business qualifications, who are known to be in favor of public education, who shall serve for two years from date of their appointment as committeemen, and until their successors are elected and qualified. If a vacancy should occur at any time by death, resignation or otherwise, it shall be the duty of the County Board of Education to fill such vacancy. And in the case aforesaid all the powers and duties conferred under this act on the Township Committeemen shall vest in the said committeemen of the several schools of the township, and they shall serve without compensation.

Qualifications.
Term of office.
Vacancy, how filled.
Powers and duties.
To serve without compensation.

NOTE.—It is left with the County Board of Education whether they will appoint a Township Committee of three, who will act for the township, or a School Committee of three for each school in the township. While the law will allow the appointment of a School Committee of three for one township in a county, and the appointment of a School Committee of three for each school in another township of the same county, it will no doubt be better to have the system uniform throughout the county.

SEC. 18. The School Committee as soon as practicable after their election and qualification not to exceed twenty days, shall meet and elect from their number a chairman and secretary, and shall keep a record of their proceedings in a book to be kept for that purpose; the name and address of the chairman and secretary shall be reported to the County Superintendent of Schools and recorded by him, and all appeals from the committee shall be first made to the County Superintendent of Schools, whose decisions shall be final, unless reversed by the County Board of Education.

School Committee shall elect Chairman and Secretary.
Record of proceedings.
To report names of Chairman and Secretary to County Superintendent.
Appeals from Committee.

NOTE.—This section requires the official acts of the committee to be done in a business manner and records kept in a book for that purpose. This is in strong contrast with the haphazard, careless way of many committees.

SEC. 19. The School Committee shall be intrusted with the care and custody of all school-houses, school-house sites, grounds, books, apparatus, or other public school property in the township with full power to control the same as they may deem best for the interest of the public schools and the cause of education.

Committee to have control of school property.

SEC. 20. The School Committee is required to furnish the County Superintendent of Schools a census report of all the pupils of school age in their township or district by name, age, sex and race, also name of parent or guardian, and the blanks upon which said reports are to be made shall be furnished to the various school committees by the County Superintendent of Schools on the first Monday in August in each year, which report shall be duly verified under oath by the committee and returned to the County Superintendent of Schools on or before the first Monday in September of each year, and any committee failing to comply with the provisions of this section without just cause shall be subject to removal. The School Committee shall be allowed a sum not exceeding two cents per name for all names reported between the ages of six and twenty-one. The School Committee shall also report to the County Superintendent of Schools who shall in turn report to the County Board of Education, the number of public school-houses and the value of all public school property for each race separately and furnish to the teacher at the opening of the school a register containing the name and age of each pupil of school age in that district. They shall also report by race and sex the number of all persons between the ages of twelve and twenty-one who can not read and write. School Committee shall meet at convenient times and places for the employment of teachers for the public schools, and no teacher shall be employed by any committee except at a regularly called meeting of

Committee to furnish County Superintendent census of children of school age, etc.

Blanks to be furnished. When.

Report to be verified.

When returnable.

Penalty for failure to comply with provisions of this section.

Compensation for making census.

Report of number of public school houses and value of school property.

List of persons of school age to be furnished teachers.

Report of persons unable to read and write.

Employment of teachers.

such committee, due notice of said meeting having been given at three public places with [by] the committee.

NOTE.—This census must be made promptly at the time and in form and contain the information required by this section. Attention is called to the manner of employing teachers.

Committee to keep itemized statement of moneys apportioned, received and expended. also copy of contracts with teachers
Power to purchase supplies.

SEC. 21. The School Committee shall keep a book in which shall be recorded an itemized statement of all moneys apportioned to, received and expended by them for each school and a copy of all contracts made by them with teachers. The committee shall have authority to purchase the supplies necessary for conducting the schools and for repairs to an amount not to exceed in the aggregate the sum of twenty-five dollars in any one year for each school.

NOTE.—The Superintendent should not recommend payment of any account against the school fund, except upon an itemized statement sworn to by the committee.

Power to employ and dismiss teachers
Time of contract.
Amount of consideration limited.
Restriction on employment.
Age limit for certificate.
Compensation allowed to teachers.
Restrictions as to third grade certificates.

SEC. 22. The School Committee shall have authority to employ and dismiss teachers, but no contract shall be made during any year to extend beyond the term of office of the committee, nor for more money than accrues to the credit of the district for the fiscal year during which the contract is made. No person shall be employed as a teacher who does not produce a certificate from the County Superintendent of Schools or other parties authorized by law to issue the same and dated within the time prescribed by law and continuing to the end of the term. No certificate to teach school shall be issued to any person under eighteen years of age. Teachers of second grade shall receive not more than twenty-five dollars per month out of the public fund, and teachers of first grade may receive such compensation as shall be agreed upon. Teachers of the third grade shall receive not more than twenty dollars per month, but no third-grade certificate shall be renewed and no holder of a third-grade certificate shall be employed except as an assistant teacher. No teacher shall receive any compensation for a shorter term than one month unless providentially hindered from completing the term. Twenty school days of not less than six hours nor more than seven hours each day shall be a month. The school term shall be continued [continuous] as far as practicable. Certificates issued by any institution as now provided by law shall be void whenever the person holding said certificate shall for three consecutive years fail to teach in some school in the State.

<small>Minimum time of compensation.
School month defined.
School term to be continued.
When certificates issued by institutions void.</small>

NOTE.—Subject to section 24, as to teachers' salary.

SEC. 23. At the end of every term of a public school, the teacher or principal of the school shall exhibit to the School Committee a statement of the number of pupils, male and female, the average daily attendance, the length of term and the time taught. If the committee is satisfied that the provisions of this act have been complied with they shall give an order on the Treasurer of the county school fund, payable to said teacher, for the full amount due for services rendered, but monthly statements shall be made by the teacher to the committee, orders on the Treasurer shall be valid when signed by two members of the committee and countersigned by the County Superintendent. When a monthly report of any school where the district does not contain over one hundred and fifty children shows an average daily attendance of less than one-fifth of the school census, the committee shall at once order the school to be closed and the money due said school shall remain to the credit of that school.

<small>At end of term teacher to exhibit statement to School Committee. Contents.
Committee to give order on Treasurer for teacher's salary.
Monthly statements of teacher.
When orders on Treasurer valid.
When Committee may order school closed, etc.</small>

SEC. 24. The County Board of Education shall on the second Monday in January and the second Monday in July of each year apportion the school fund of the county to the various townships in said county per capita; but

<small>Apportionment of school fund, when.</small>

School Law——2

18

How.
Contingent fund first reserved.
For what purpose.

they shall before apportioning the school fund to the various townships, reserve as a contingent fund an amount sufficient to pay the salary of the County Superintendent and per diem and expenses of the County Board of Education and other necessary expenses. It shall be the duty of

School funds to be apportioned so as to equalize terms of schools if possible.

the County Board of Education to distribute and apportion the school money of each township so as to give to each school in said township for each race the same length of school term, as nearly as may be each year, and in making such apportionments the said County Board of Education shall have proper regard for the grade of work

Must take into consideration grade of work and qualifications of teachers required.
Maximum salary to be fixed.

to be done and the qualifications of the teachers required in each school for each race and the said County Board of Education shall fix the maximum salary for each school in the county. As soon as the apportionments are made it shall be the duty of the County Board of Education to

School Committeemen and Treasurer to be notified of apportionment.
Schools, how numbered.

notify the School Committeemen and the treasurer of the county school fund of the amount apportioned to each school, and each school shall be designated as school No. 1, 2, 3, etc., for white, colored, or Indian, in .... Township, in the county of ....

NOTE.—The general expenses authorized are Treasurer's commission, mileage, and per diem of County Board of Education, Salary of County Superintendent, and other necessary expenses.

Semi annual apportionment, what based upon.

SEC. 25. The semi-annual apportionment of public school moneys shall be based upon the amounts actually received by the County Treasurer from all sources and reported by him to the County Board of Education as required by this act.

Appropriations for conducting teachers' institutes.

SEC. 26. The County Board of Education of any county may annually appropriate an amount not exceeding one hundred dollars out of the school funds of the county for the purpose of conducting one or more Teachers' Institutes for said county or the County Boards of Education of two or more adjoining counties may appropriate an amount not exceeding one hundred dollars to each county, for the purpose of conducting a Teachers' Institute for said counties at some convenient and satisfactory point. All teach- *Teachers required to attend.* ers of any county in which such institute is held are hereby required to attend the same continuously during the session thereof; and, upon failure to do so, unless providentially hindered, shall be debarred from teaching in any of the public schools of this State for the term of one year, *Penalty for failure.* or until such teacher shall have attended some county institute in some other county. A county Teachers' Institute under this section shall be conducted by the County *By whom conducted.* Superintendent of Schools, assisted by some member of the State Board of Examiners, or a member of the faculty of the Normal Department of the University of North Carolina, or of the State Normal and Industrial College, or of the Agricultural and Mechanical College at Raleigh, or by some practical teacher or teachers appointed by the State Superintendent of Public Instruction.

NOTE.—A County Teachers' Institute shall be conducted by the County Superintendent. Teachers are required to attend continuously, upon penalty of being *debarred* from teaching.

SEC. 27. The County Board of Education shall meet *When County Board to meet.* on the second Monday in January, April, July and October and [m]ay, if necessary, continue in session two days and they may have called meetings, of one day each, as often as once a month if the school business of the county requires it. They shall receive the same per diem *Mileage and per diem.* and mileage as that allowed the County Commissioners, and shall at the meeting in January, April, July and October, examine the books and vouchers, audit the accounts of *Duties and powers.* treasurer of the county school fund and shall have power to fix the maximum monthly salary for first-grade teachers.

SEC. 28. The County Board of Education of each *Power to punish for contempt.*

county shall have power to punish for contempt, for any disorderly conduct or disturbance tending to interrupt them in the transaction of their official business, and every person who shall wilfully interrupt or disturb any public or private school or any meeting lawfully and peacefully held for the purpose of literary and scientific improvement, either within or without the place where such meeting or school is held, or injure any school building, or deface any school furniture, apparatus, or other school property, shall be guilty of a misdemeanor and fined not exceeding fifty dollars or imprisoned not more than thirty days. Any person who shall wilfully set fire to any schoolhouse or procure the same to be done shall be guilty of a misdemeanor, and upon conviction shall be punished by imprisonment in the penitentiary or the county jail, and may also be fined in the discretion of the Court.

SEC. 29. The County Board of Education shall divide the townships into convenient school districts as compact in form as practicable. They shall consult the convenience and necessities of each race in setting the boundaries of the school district for each race, and shall establish no new school in any township within less than three miles by the nearest traveled route of some school already established in said township; nor shall they create any school district with less than sixty-five children of school age, unless prevented by geographical reason or sparsely settled neighborhoods. Nothing in this act shall prevent the Board of Education, whenever they shall deem it necessary for the good of the public schools, from forming a school district out of portions of two or more contiguous townships.

NOTE.—The County Board of Education should combine and consolidate the schools, in most instances making fewer and better schools. This end should be kept in view in making the boundaries. One school with two teachers is better than two schools. If you increase the number of schools you shorten the terms.

SEC. 30. The County Board of Education may receive any gift, grant, donation or devise made for the use of any school or schools within their jurisdiction. When, in the opinion of the board, any school-house, school-house site, or other public school property has become unnecessary for public purposes, they may sell the same at public auction, after advertisement of twenty days at three public places in the county, or at private sale. The deed for the property thus sold shall be executed by the chairman and clerk of the board, and the proceeds of the sale shall be paid to the treasurer of the county school fund. *Power to receive gifts, dispose of school property, etc. Deed, how executed.*

SEC. 31. The County Board of Education may receive suitable sites for school-houses by donation or purchase. In case of purchase they shall issue an order on the treasurer of the County Board of Education for the purchase-money and upon payment of the order the title to the said site shall vest in the board and their successors in office. Whenever the board is unable to obtain a suitable site for a school by gift or purchase, they shall report to the County Superintendent of County Instruction, who shall, upon five days' notice to the owner of the land, apply to the Clerk of the Superior Court for the appointment of three appraisers, who shall lay off, by metes and bounds, not more than one acre, and assess the value thereof. They shall make a written report of their proceedings, to be signed by them, or by a majority of them, to the said Clerk within five days from their appointment, who shall enter the same upon the records of the Court. Said appraisers and officers shall serve without compensation. If said report is confirmed by the Clerk of the Court, the chairman and secretary shall issue an order on the treasurer of the County Board of Education in favor of the owner of the land thus laid off, and upon the payment or offer of payment of this order the title to said land shall vest in the County Board and their successors in office. *Disposal of proceeds. Sites for school-houses. Title, in whom vested. Procedure to condemn sites where unable to purchase, and assess damages. Upon payment or offer of payment title to vest in County Boards and their successors.*

22

Provisions as to improved land. Improved land shall not be condemned under this section unless it be essential to secure a proper location. Any **Appeal.** person aggrieved by the action of said appraisers may appeal to the Superior Court of the county in which the land is situated upon giving bond to secure the board **Appeal bond.** against such costs as may be incurred on account of said appeal not being prosecuted with effect.

Deeds to be recorded and kept by Clerk of Court. SEC. 32. All deeds to the County Board of Education shall be recorded and delivered to the Clerk of the Court for safe keeping.

Contracts with teachers of private schools, when made, etc. SEC. 33. In any school district where there may be a private school, regularly conducted for at least six months in the year the School Committee may contract with the teacher of such private school to give instructions to all pupils between the ages of six and twenty-one years in the branches of learning taught in the public schools, as prescribed in this act, without charge and free of tuition; and **Compensation.** such School Committee may pay such teacher for such service out of the public school fund apportioned to the district and the agreement as to such pay shall be arranged between the committee and teacher. Every teacher of the **Qualifications of such teachers.** public school branches in said school shall obtain a first-grade certificate before beginning his or her work, and **Reports.** shall from time to time make such reports as are required of other school teachers under this act. The County Su**Authority of County Superintendent.** perintendents of Schools have the same authority in respect to the employment and dismissal of teachers under this section, and in every other respect as is conferred in **Contracts to designate minimum public school term.** other sections of the law. And all contracts made under this section shall designate the minimum length of the public school term, which shall not be less than the average length of the public school term of the county of the **Maximum amount to be paid private school fixed.** preceding year. The amount paid said private school for each pupil in the public school branches, based on the aver-

23

age daily attendance, shall not exceed the regular tuition rates in said school for said branches of study.

NOTE.—If the tuition in the private school for the public school branches is $1.00 or $2.00 per month, then said private school shall not be allowed any more per capita of the public fund than they receive per capita from the parents in the private funds. To illustrate: If there are forty children in the public school branches whose private tuition is $40.00, then the committee can only pay $40.00 per month for this instruction out of the public fund.

SEC. 34. No contract for teachers' salaries shall be made during any fiscal year for a larger amount of money than accrues to the credit of the respective districts for the year, and no committee shall give an order unless the money to pay it is actually to the credit of the district, and no part of the school fund for one year shall be used to pay school claims for any previous year. *Amount of contracts restricted. Restriction on Committee in giving orders. Restriction on use of annual school fund.*

NOTE.—The great number of special acts for payments of teachers' salaries by the last Legislature is the result of a disregard of this section.

SEC. 35. The School Committee for each township shall keep a book in which shall be kept an itemized account of all moneys apportioned, received and expended by them for each school and a copy of all contracts made by them with teachers. *School Committee to keep account of moneys and contracts.*

NOTE.—The County Board of Education will require a literal compliance with this section of the law.

SEC. 36. The County Superintendent of Schools shall be *ex officio* the Secretary of the County Board of Education. He shall record all proceedings of the Board of Education, issue all notices and orders that may be made by said board pertaining to the public schools, school-houses, sites, or districts, (which notices or orders it shall be the duty of *County Superintendent ex officio Secretary of County Board of Education.*

Duties.

t(,e secretary to serve by mail or by personal delivery without cost), and record all school statistics, look after all forfeitures, fines and penalties, see that the same are placed to the credit of the school fund and report the same to the County Board of Education.

County Board to provide office for County Superintendent at county seat, also record book.

The County Board of Education shall provide the County Superintendent of Schools with an office at the county seat and with a suitable book in which to keep the records required by this section. The record of the Board of Education and the County Superintendent of Schools shall be kept in the office provided for that purpose by the said board.

Record, where kept.

NOTE.—The duties of Superintendent as Secretary of *County Board of Education* are very important.

Examination of teachers, where and when conducted.

SEC. 37. The County Superintendent of Schools of each county shall examine all applicants of good moral character for teacher's certificate at the court-house in the county, on the second Thursday of July and October of every year, and continue the examination from day to day during the remainder of the week, if necessary, till all applicants are examined, and for the examination of teachers at any other time than above named he shall require of such applicant a fee of one dollar, in advance, and all fees for private examination shall be paid by the County Superintendent of Schools to the treasurer of the county school fund to go to the general school fund of the county. The place for holding the examination of teachers shall be at the county seat, but other places in said county may be designated by the County Superintendent of Schools, when, in his discretion, it may be for the convenience of the teachers of his county. A general average of ninety per centum and over shall entitle an applicant to a first-grade certificate; a general average of eighty per centum or more shall entitle the applicant to a second grade certificate; and a general average of seventy shall entitle an

Fee.

Fees for private examination, how disposed of.

Place for holding examination.

What per cent entitles to first-grade certificate.

What entitles to second-grade certificate

What entitles to third-grade certificate.

applicant to a third-grade certificate. The certificates shall be valid only in the county in which they are issued and for one year from date, except that first-grade certificates shall be valid for two years. The branches taught in the public schools shall be orthography, defining [reading], writing, drawing, arithmetic geography, grammar, language lessons, history of North Carolina, including the Constitution of the State, history of the United States, including the Constitution of the United States, physiology, hygiene, nature and effect of alcoholic drinks and narcotics, elements of civil government, elements of agriculture, theory and practice of teaching, and such other branches as the State Board of Education may direct. The County Superintendent of Schools shall hold his examinations publicly, and may invite competent persons to assist him in such examination. He shall keep a copy of all examination questions, both public and private, and forward copies to the State Superintendent upon request. No Superintendent shall renew any second-grade certificate, except upon re-examination. *(Certificates, how long and where valid. List of branches to be taught in public schools. Examinations public. Copies to be kept and forwarded to State Superintendent on request.)*

SEC. 38. The County Superintendent shall each year hold not less than one teachers' meeting in each township, which the teachers shall be required to attend, if necessary one-half of a school day may be set apart for this purpose. *(Teachers' meetings.)*

SEC. 39. It shall be the duty of the County Superintendent to advise with the teachers as to the best methods of instruction and school government, and to that end he shall keep himself thoroughly informed as to the progress of education in other counties, cities and States; he shall have authority to correct abuses, and to this end he may, with the concurrence of a majority of the School Committee, suspend any teacher who may be guilty of any immoral or disreputable conduct, or may prove himself incompetent to discharge efficiently the duties of a public *(Duties and powers of County Superintendent. Suspension of teachers.)*

school teacher, or who may be persistently neglectful of said duties. The County Superintendent shall be required to visit the public schools of his county while in session under the direction of the County Board of Education, and shall inform himself of the condition and needs for [of] the various schools within his jurisdiction.

To visit public schools, etc

NOTE.—The duties prescribed by this section are mandatory, and can only be faithfully performed where the County Boards of Education will make liberal provision for the Superintendent.

Duties of County Superintendent. To distribute blanks.

SEC. 40. It shall be the duty of the County Superintendent of the Schools to distribute to the various School Committees of his county all such blanks as may be furnished by the State Superintendent of Public Instruction for reports of school statistics of the several districts; also, blanks for teachers' reports and for orders on the treasurer of the county school fund for teachers' salaries;

To distribute school registers.

he shall also distribute to the School Committees school registers for their respective districts and necessary record book; he shall advise with said committee as to the best

Advise as to gathering and reporting school statistics.

methods of gathering the school statistics contemplated by such blanks, and, by all proper means, shall seek to have such statistics fully and properly reported.

Duty of County Superintendent to report to State Superintendent Public Instruction on or before July 1st every year.

SEC. 41. It shall be the duty of the County Superintendent of Schools in each county, on or before the first Monday in July of every year, to report to the State Superintendent of Public Instruction an abstract statement of the number, grade, race, and sex of the teachers examined and approved by him during the year; also, the

Contents of report.

number of public schools taught in the county during the year for each race; the number of children of school age in each school district; the number enrolled in each district; the average daily attendance in each district by race and sex and the number of all persons in the county between the ages of twelve and twenty-one who can not read and write. He shall also report by race and sex the number of pupils of each race enrolled in all the schools, their average attendance; the average length of terms of said schools, and the average salary, respectively, for the teachers of each race; the number of school districts for each race, and any new school districts laid out during the year shall be specified in his report. He shall also report the number of public school-houses and the value of the public school property for each race; the number of Teachers' Institutes held; the number of teachers attending such institutes, together with such suggestions as may occur to him promotive of the school interest of the county. The County Superintendent of the Schools shall record in his book an accurate copy of his report to the State Superintendent of Public Instruction. If any County Superintendent of Schools fails or refuses to perform any of the duties required of him by this act he shall be subject to removal from his office by the County Board of Education upon the complaint of the State Superintendent of Public Instruction. *County Superintendent to record in his book copy of his report.* *Failure of County Superintendent to perform any duties subject to removal from office.*

NOTE.—This report must be held by County Superintendent for review by County Board of Education on second Monday of July. (See section 59.)

SEC. 42. In case the County Superintendent shall have sufficient evidence at any time that any member of the committee is not capable of discharging, or is not discharging, the duties of his office, he shall bring the matter to the attention of the County Board of Education, which shall thoroughly investigate the charges and shall remove said committeeman and appoint a successor if sufficient evidence shall be produced to warrant his removal and the best interest of the schools demand it. *Incapacity or failure of Committeemen to discharge official duties cause for removal.* *Procedure.*

NOTE.—This is a delicate and often unpleasant duty, but the best interest of the schools demands it.

SEC. 43. That it shall be the duty of the County Superintendent of Public Instruction to require of the School Committee, in enumerating the number of school children, to make a statement in the report of the number of deaf, dumb and blind between the ages of six and twenty-one years, designating the race and sex, and the address of the parent or guardian of said children; and the County Superintendents of Public Instruction are hereby required to furnish such information to the principals of the deaf, dumb and blind institutions, and the Superintendent of Public Instruction, in preparing blanks, as directed in The Code, sec. 3370, shall include questions, answers to which will furnish the information as aforesaid.

List of deaf, dumb and blind children.
To be furnished Superintendent of Deaf, Dumb and Blind Institutions.
Blanks to contain questions relative thereto.

SEC. 44. The compensation of the County Superintendent of Schools shall be not less than two dollars, nor more than three dollars per diem, or the Board of Education may pay an annual compensation to the County Superintendent not to exceed four per cent of the disbursements for the schools under his supervision. Every County Superintendent shall reside in the county of which he is Superintendent. It shall not be lawful for any County Superintendent to teach a school while the public schools of his county are in session: *Provided,* the State Board of Education may, for good and sufficient reason, permit a County Superintendent to so teach.

Compensation of County Superintendent of Schools.
Residence of County Superintendent. Unlawful to teach school.
Proviso.

NOTE.—This section is alternative, giving as pay to County Superintendent a per diem of not less than $2.00, nor more than $3.00, or instead thereof, 4 per cent of disbursements for schools under his charge, to be decided by County Board of Education.

SEC. 45. The members of the County Board of Education, the School Committeemen and the County Superintendent of Schools in each county shall, before entering upon the duties of their office, take oath for the faithful performance thereof.

Oath of office.

SEC. 46. The County Treasurer of each county shall receive and disburse all public school funds, and shall keep the same separate and distinct from all other funds, but before entering upon the duties of his office he shall execute a justified Treasurer's bond, with security in an amount to be fixed by the Board of County Commissioners in an amount not less than the moneys received by him or by his predecessor during the previous year, conditioned for the faithful performance of his duties as treasurer of the county school fund, and for the payment over to his successor in office of any balance of school moneys that may be in his hands unexpended, and the County Board of Commissioners may, from time to time, if necessary, require him to strengthen said bond, and in default thereof the members of the County Board of Commissioners shall be guilty of a misdemeanor. *County Treasurer to receive and disburse school funds. To keep same seperate. To execute bond. Amount. Conditions of bond. Increase of bond Concerning default of County Commissioners.*

SEC. 47. The bond of the Treasurer of the county school fund shall be approved by the Board of County Commissioners, and they shall bring action for any breach thereof, and on their failure to bring such action it may be brought in the name of the State on the relation of any tax-payer. The said bond shall be separate, not including liabilities for other funds. *Approval of Treasurer's bond. Action by whom brought. Separate bond.*

SEC. 48. All orders for the payment of teachers' salaries, for building, repairs, school furnishings, or for the payment of money for any purpose whatsoever, before it shall be a valid voucher in the hand of the County Treasurer, shall be signed first by at least two members of the committee, then by the County Superintendent. No order shall be signed by the County Superintendent for more money than is to the credit of that district for the fiscal year, nor shall Superintendent of Schools endorse the order of any teacher who does not produce a certificate as required in section 22. The said treasurer shall not pay any school money for building or repairing any *When orders shall be valid, vouchers in hands of Treasurer. Limit to amount of order. Restriction as to endorsement of teacher's order.*

school-house unless the site on which it is located has been donated to or purchased by the County Board of Education and the deed for the same regularly executed and delivered to said board, and their successors in office, probated, registered in the office of the Register of Deeds for the county and delivered to the Clerk of the Court, to be by him safely deposited with his valuable official papers, and surrendered to his successor in office and for default he shall be liable on his official bond for any sum thus illegally paid.

<small>Order for building and repairs not to be paid till title passed, registered and deposited with clerk.</small>

<small>Treasurer liable on bond for sums illegally paid.</small>

SEC. 49. It shall be the duty of the treasurer of the county school fund to keep a book in which he shall open an account with each township in the county, showing the amount apportioned to the various townships by the County Board of Education. He shall also open an account with each school district showing the amount apportioned to various school districts. He shall record the date of all payments of school money in the name of the person to whom paid and for what purpose and the several amounts. He shall balance the amount of each township and district annually on the thirtieth of June of each year, and shall report by letter or printed circular, within ten days thereafter, said balances to the County Board of Education and to the School Committee.

<small>Treasurer's school account books, what to show.</small>

<small>To balance accounts annually.</small>

<small>To report balance to County Board and School Committee.</small>

SEC. 50. The treasurer of the county school fund shall when required by the County Board of Education produce his books and vouchers for examination, and shall also exhibit all moneys due the public school fund of the county at each settlement required by this act.

<small>Treasurer, when required to produce books, vouchers and exhibit school moneys at settlements.</small>

SEC. 51. The Treasurer of the county school fund of each county shall report to the State Superintendent of Public Instruction on the first Monday of August of each year the entire amount of money received and disbursed by him during the preceding school year, designated by items, the amounts received respectively from property

<small>Treasurer's report to State Superintendent of Public Instruction.</small>

<small>When made.</small>

<small>Contents.</small>

tax, poll tax, liquor licenses, fines, forfeitures, and penalties, auctioneers, estrays, from State Treasurer and from other sources. He shall also designate by item the sum paid to teachers of each race respectively, for schoolhouses, school sites in the several districts, and for all other purposes specifically, and in detail, by item, and on the same date he shall file a duplicate of said report in the office of the County Board of Education. He shall make such other reports as the County Board of Education of the county may require from time to time. *Duplicate report to be filed with County Board of Education. Other reports.*

SEC. 52. The treasurer of the county school fund shall keep a book in which shall be entered a full and detailed account of all public school moneys received by him, the name of each person paying him school money, the source from which the same may have been derived, and the date of such payment. In his settlement with the Sheriff or other collecting officer of public school funds the said treasurer shall receive money only. *Treasurer's account of receipts. To receive money only from Sheriff or other collecting officer.*

SEC. 53. Any treasurer of the county school fund failing to make reports required of him at the time and in the manner prescribed, or to perform any other duties required of him in this act shall be guilty of a misdemeanor and be fined not less than fifty dollars and not more than two hundred dollars, or imprisoned not less than thirty days, nor more than six months, in the discretion of the Court. *Misdemeanor for Treasurer to fail to do any duty required in this act. Penalty.*

SEC. 54. The Sheriff of each county shall pay annually in money to the treasurer of the county school fund on or before the thirty-first day of December of each year, the whole amount levied, less such sum or sums as may be allowed on account of insolvents for the current year, by both State and county, for school purposes, and on failing to do so shall be guilty of a misdemeanor and fined not less than two hundred dollars, and be liable to an action on his official bond for his default in such sum as will *Sheriff to settle school funds in money with Treasurer on or before December 1 in each year. Failu es misdemeanor. Penalties.*

cover such default, said action to be brought to the next ensuing term of the Superior Court, and upon the relation of the County Commissioners for and in behalf of the State.

Action on bond, how brought.

NOTE.—The only sum deducted from the "whole amount levied by both State and county for school purposes will be that allowed on account of insolvents for the current year."

Sheriff to take from Treasurer duplicate receipts.

To whom transmitted.

Failure a misdemeanor. Penalty.

SEC. 55. The Sheriff or other collecting officer shall take duplicate receipt of the treasurer of the county school fund for such payment as he may make under this act, one copy of which shall be transmitted to the Auditor of the State and one to the chairman of the County Board of Education, and upon his failure to do so he shall be guilty of a misdemeanor and fined or imprisoned as in section 53 of this act.

Items to be designated in payments and receipts.

SEC. 56. Whenever the Sheriff or other collecting officer pays over money to the treasurer of the school fund he shall designate the items as indicated in section 51 of this act, and these items shall be stated in the receipts given by the treasurer.

When office of Treasurer expires.

When he vacates his office during fiscal school year, to file report.

What to contain.

This report to be included in his successor's report.

SEC. 57. If the term of office of any treasurer shall expire on the thirtieth day of November during any fiscal school year, or if for any reason he shall hold office beyond the thirtieth day of November, and not for the whole of the current fiscal school year, he shall, at the time he goes out of office, file with the County Board of Education and with his successors a report, itemized, as required by section 51 of this act, covering the receipts and disbursements for that part of the fiscal school year from the thirtieth of June preceding to the time at which he turns over the office to his successor, and his successor shall include in his report to the State Superintendent the receipts and disbursements for the current fiscal year.

SEC. 58. Each treasurer of the county school fund in going out of office, shall deposit in the office of the Board of Education of his county his books, in which are kept his school accounts, and all records and blanks pertaining to his office. The treasurer of the county school fund shall, on the last Saturday of each month, attend at his office for the purpose of paying school orders; but this shall not be construed to prevent the payment of orders at other times; and he shall be allowed for compensation as treasurer of the school fund such sum as the Board of Education may allow him, not to exceed two per centum of his vouchers paid on orders of School Committees. *Retiring Treasurer to deposit books, records and blanks, where.* *When school orders paid.* *Compensation of Treasurer.*

SEC. 59. On the second Monday of July, the County Board of Education, County Superintendent of Schools and Treasurer shall meet at the office of the board and settle all the business of the preceding fiscal year. The board shall on that day examine the reports of Treasurer and County Superintendent, and if found correct shall direct them to be forwarded. *Annual settlement of school business.* *Examination and forwarding books of Treasurer and County Superintendent.*

SEC. 60. The Auditor of the State shall include on the form which he furnishes to the Board of County Commissioners and on which the tax lists are to be made out, separate columns for school poll tax and school property tax, in one of which columns the total poll tax levied by the General Assembly and the county authorities for schools due by each tax-payer and in the other the total property tax levied by the General Assembly on [and] the county authorities for schools due by each tax-payer. *Revised form of blanks for tax lists to be sent out by Auditor.*

SEC. 61. The Register of Deeds shall furnish to the County Board of Education, as soon as the tax lists are made out, an abstract of said lists, showing in separate columns the total amount of poll tax borne on said lists, and also the total amount of property tax borne on the same, and shall furnish such other information from his office as the County Board of Education may require. *Register of Deeds to furnish County Boards of Education abstract of tax lists.* *What to show.* *Other information.*

NOTE.—This is a very important section of the school law to school officers.

34

Clerks of courts to furnish County Boards statement of fines, penalties and forfeitures going to school fund, when.

SEC. 62. The Clerks of all Criminal, Superior and Municipal Courts shall furnish to the County Board of Education of the county on the first Monday of July and January of each year a detailed statement of fines, forfeitures and penalties which go to the school fund that have been imposed, or which have accrued. Any Clerk failing to comply with the duties herein prescribed shall be guilty of a misdemeanor, and shall, upon conviction, be fined or imprisoned in the discretion of the Court.

Failure a misdemeanor. Penalty.

Duties of teachers in schools.

SEC. 63. It shall be the duty of all teachers of free public schools to maintain good order and discipline in their respective schools; to encourage morality, industry and neatness in all of their pupils, and to teach thoroughly all branches which they are required to teach. Pupils who wilfully and persistently violate the rules of the school and any of immoral life and character shall be dismissed by the teacher.

Dismissal of pupils.

Teachers to keep daily record.

SEC. 64. Every teacher or principal of a school to which aid shall be given under this act shall keep a daily record of the attendance of pupils. At the end of every term every principal or teacher of a public school shall report to the County Superintendent of Schools the length of term of school, the race for which it was taught, the number, the sex, and average daily attendance of the pupils, and the number of the district in which the school is taught, the number of children on census blank not attending any school this year, number of children under seventeen years of age not attending any school; state some causes why they do not attend, how many families having children of school age did not send any of their children to school, how many families did; state what personal effort you have made to get these children to attend school; number of children studying primary arithmetic, number studying intermediate arithmetic, number studying advanced arithmetic, number studying primary geog-

Report of teachers to County Superintendent, what to contain.

raphy, number studying intermediate geography, number studying language lessons, number studying elementary English grammar, number studying higher English grammar, number studying elementary history of North Carolina, number studying advanced history of North Carolina, number studying elementary history of United States, number studying higher history of United States, number studying elementary physiology and hygiene, number studying advanced physiology and hygiene, number studying civil government, number studying Latin, number studying algebra, number studying higher English. Teachers shall file with their Registers at the end of the school term an accurate record of the promotion, advancement, and classification of every child attending the school just closed. *Teachers to file record at end of school. Contents.*

NOTE.—The personal effort made by the teachers to secure accurate information required will greatly facilitate his work in the school and add to our fund of reliable statistics. The County Superintendents should not approve the voucher of any teacher who does not intelligently furnish this information.

SEC. 65. Every school to which aid shall be given under this act shall be a public school to which all children living within the district between the ages of six and twenty-one years shall be admitted free of charge for tuition. The committee may admit pay students over twenty-one years of age. *What constitutes public school. Children of school age admitted free. Pay students.*

SEC. 66. The principal or superintendent of every school or institution of learning supported in whole or in part by public funds shall report to the State Superintendent at such time and in such form as he may direct. *Principal or Superintendent of sch ol sup ported wholly or partly by public funds to report to State Superintendent.*

SEC. 67. The fiscal school year shall begin on the first day of July and close on the thirtieth of June next succeeding. *Fiscal school year.*

NOTE.—The school year begins on the first day of July. No scuool shall be in session at close of fiscal year; i. e., the term can not embrace parts of two school years.

36

Section 1810 of Code to govern right of child to attend school.

SEC. 68. In determining the right of any child to attend the schools of either race, the rule laid down in section 1810 of The Code, regulating marriages, shall be followed.

Restriction on purchase of school supplies.

SEC. 69. It shall be unlawful for any County Board of Education or School Committee to buy school supplies in which any member has a pecuniary interest. Nor shall any school officers or teachers receive any gift, emolument, *On recommendation, etc., of school supplies.* reward or promise of reward for influence in recommending or procuring the use of any school supplies for the *Violation a misdemeanor.* schools with which they are connected. Any person violating the provisions of this act shall be removed from his *To be removed from office.* position in the public service and shall, upon conviction, be deemed guilty of a misdemeanor.

State Board of Examiners and by whom elected.

SEC. 70. The State Board of Education shall elect biennially a State Board of Examiners, which shall consist *Of whom to consist.* of three professional teachers and the State Superintendent of Public Instruction, who shall be *ex officio* the chairman of said board. The said Board of Examiners shall have the entire management and control of the Col- *Powers and duties.* ored Normal Schools of the State, shall prepare a course of study for the same, elect teachers therein, fix all salaries and provide for Summer School of not less than two weeks' duration, which all teachers in said Normal School *One member to visit Colored Normal School and report.* shall be required to attend. One member of said Board of Examiners shall visit each of said Colored Normal Schools annually, inspect the work and report in writing to the State Superintendent of Public Instruction, who *Reports printed and submitted to General Assembly.* shall have the reports printed and submitted to the General Assembly on or before January twentieth, 1903. *Meetings of Board of Examiners, when held.* Meetings of the State Boards of Examiners shall be held at the call of the State Superintendent of Public Instruc- *Compensation.* tion, and the members shall receive no compensation other than traveling expenses and board while attending upon their official duties, an itemized statement of which shall be kept in the books of the State Superintendent of Public Instruction.

SEC. 71. In every incorporated city or town in which there is not now levied a special tax for schools, upon a petition signed by one-fourth of the freeholders therein, the Board of Aldermen or Town Commissioners of said city or town shall, at the date of municipal or general election next ensuing upon the presentation of said petition order an election to be held to ascertain the will of the people whether there shall be levied in such city or town a special annual tax of not more than thirty cents on the one hundred dollars valuation of property and ninety cents on the poll to supplement the Public School Fund in such city or town. Said election shall be held in the different election precincts or wards under the law governing municipal or general elections in said cities or towns. At said election those who are in favor of the levy and collection of said tax shall vote a ticket on which shall be printed or written the words, "For Special Tax," and those who are opposed shall vote a ticket on which shall be printed or written the words, "Against Special Tax." In case a majority of the qualified voters at said election is in favor of said tax the same shall be annually levied and collected in such town or city in the manner prescribed for the levy and collection of other city taxes. All moneys levied under the provisions of this section shall, upon collection, be placed to the credit of the Town School Committee, composed of not less than five nor more than seven members, appointed by the Board of Aldermen for said city or town, and shall be, by said committee, expended exclusively upon the public schools in said city or town, and there shall be but one school district in the said city or town in which there may be established one or more schools for each race, and the School Committee shall apportion the money among said schools in such manner as in their judgment will equalize school facilities.

SEC. 72. Special school tax districts may be formed by the County Board of Education in any county without regard to township lines under the following conditions: Upon a petition of one-fourth of the freeholders within the proposed special school districts, endorsed by the County Board of Education, the Board of County Commissioners, after thirty days' notice at the court-house door and three other public places in the proposed district, shall hold an election to ascertain the will of the people within the proposed special school district whether there shall be levied in said district a special annual tax of not more than thirty cents on the one hundred dollars valuation of property and ninety cents on the poll to supplement the Public School Fund, which may be apportioned to said district by the County Board of Education in case such special tax is voted. Said election shall be held in the said district under the law governing general elections as near as may be. At said election those who are in favor of the levy and collection of said tax shall vote a ticket on which shall be printed or written the words, "For Special Tax," and those who are opposed shall vote a ticket on which shall be printed or written the words, "Against Special Tax." In case a majority of the qualified voters at said election is in favor of said tax the same shall be annually levied and collected in the manner prescribed for the levy and collection of other taxes. All money levied under the provisions of this act shall, upon collection be placed to the credit of the School Committee in said district, which committee shall be appointed by the County Board of Education; and the said School Committee shall apportion the money among the schools in said districts in such manner as in their judgment shall equalize school facilities.

SEC. 73. The provisions of this act shall not apply to any township, city or town now levying a special tax for schools and operating under special laws or charters, or to schools operating under section 47, chapter 199, Laws of 1889, school districts in any city or town now operating under section 47, chapter 199, Laws of 1889, are hereby continued and all vacancies in the School Committee therein shall be filled by the County Board of Education, and if said districts comprise a township there shall not be appointed township school committeemen for said township, and all apportionment shall be made directly to the committee of said districts. *Restrictions on application of this act. Vacancies in certain special school districts, how filled. Where districts comprise a township, regulations relative thereto.*

SEC. 74. Section 47, chapter 199, Laws of 1889, is hereby amended by striking out the words, "By and with the consent of the County Board of Education." *Section 47, Chapter 199, Laws 1889, amended.*

SEC. 75. That all laws and clauses of laws in conflict with the provisions of this act shall be and the same is hereby repealed. *Conflicting laws repealed.*

SEC. 76. That this act shall be in force from and after its ratification.

In the General Assembly read three times, and ratified this the 11th day of March, A. D., 1901.

An Act to amend the Public School Law, ratified March 11, 1901.

The General Assembly of North Carolina do enact:

SECTION 1. That the word "with" in line 49 of section 20, and after "places" and before "the" be stricken out and "by" inserted therefor. *Section 20 amended.*

SEC. 2. That the word "continued" after "be" and before "as" in line 38, section 22, be stricken out and "continuous" be inserted therefor. *Section 22 amended.*

SEC. 3. That the capital "M" in the word "May" after and before "if" in line 4, section 27, be changed to a small "m." *Section 27 amended.*

SEC. 4. That after *"schools"* and before *"when"* in line 24, section 37, strike out the period and insert a comma. *Section 37 amended.*

Section 41 amended.

Section 57 amended.

SEC. 5. After "subject" and before "removal" in line 46, section 41, strike out "of" and insert "to."

SEC. 6. After *"race"* and before *"for"* in line 16, section 57, strike out "respectfully" and insert "respectively."

SEC. 7. That this act shall be in force from and after its ratification.

In the General Assembly read three times, and ratified this the 15th day of March, A. D. 1901.

An Act to Establish a Text-Book Commission.

The General Assembly of North Carolina do enact:

State Board of Education constituted State Text-Book Commission Duties.

SECTION 1. That the State Board of Education, shall be and is hereby constituted a State Text-Book Commission, whose duty it is to select and adopt a uniform series or system of text-books for use in the public schools in the State of North Carolina.

To select and adopt uniform text books for public schools.

When adopted to be used five years.

Unlawful to use other books.

Branches included in uniform series.

SEC. 2. That said Commission is hereby authorized, empowered and directed to select and adopt a uniform system or series of text-books for use in the public schools of the State, as above indicated, and when so selected and adopted, the text-books shall be used for a period of five years, in all the public schools of this State, and it shall not be lawful for any school officer, director or teacher, to use any other books upon the same branches, other than those adopted by said State Text-Book Commission. Said uniform series shall include the following branches, to-wit: Orthography, defining, reading, writing, drawing, arithmetic, geography, grammar, language lessons, history of North Carolina, containing the Constitution of the State; history of the United States, containing the Constitution of the United States, physiology, hygiene, nature and effect of alcoholic drinks, and narcotics, elements of civil government, elements of agriculture, theory and practice of teaching: *Provided,* that none of said text-books shall contain anything of a partisan or sectarian character. *(Must be non-partisan.)*

SEC. 3. It shall be the duty of the Governor to appoint a sub-commission of not less than five, nor more than ten, to be selected from among the teachers, or city or county superintendents, actually engaged in the school business in this State: *Provided,* that not more than two of these shall be taken from and Congressional District, to whom shall be referred all books sent to the State Text-Book Commission as specimen copies or samples, upon which bids are to be based, and it shall be the duty of said sub-commmission, in executive session, to examine and report upon the merits of the books, irrespective of the price, taking into consideration the subject-matter of the books, their printing, their material, and their mechanical qualities, and their general suitability and desirability for the purposes for which they are desired and intended. *(Governor to appoint Sub-Commission. Number. Who eligible. Location. Duties of Sub-Commission.)*

SEC. 4. That it shall further be the duty of said sub-commission to report to the Commission at such time as said Commission shall direct, arranging each book in its class, or division, and reporting them in the order of their merit, pointing out the merits and demerits of each book, and indicating what book they recommend for adoption first, what book is their second choice, and their third choice, and so on, pursuing this plan with the books submitted upon each branch of study, and if said sub-commission shall consider different books upon the same subject, or of the same class or division of approximately even merit, all things being considered, they shall so report, and if they consider that any of the books offered are of such a class as to make them inferior and not worthy of adoption, they shall, in their report, so designate such books, and in said report they shall make such recommendations and suggestion to the Commission as they shall deem advisable and proper to make. Said report shall be kept secret and sealed up, and delivered to the secretary *(Sub Commission to report to Commission. What report to contain. Report kept secret and delivered to Secretary of Commission.)*

of the Commission, and said report shall not be opened by any member of the Commission until the Commission shall meet in executive session to open and consider the bids, or proposals, of publishers, or others, desiring to have books adopted by said Commission.

When opened.

SEC. 5. That each member of said sub-commission, before entering upon the discharge of his duties, shall take and subscribe an oath to act honestly, conscientiously, and faithfully, and that he is not now, and has not within two years prior to his appointment, been agent or attorney, or in the employment of, or interested in, any book, or publishing house, concern, or corporation, making, or proposing to make, bids for the sale of books, pursuant to the provisions of this act; and that he will examine all books submitted carefully and faithfully, and make true report thereon, as herein directed and prescribed. Said oath shall be filed in the office of the Secretary of State.

Oath of Sub-Commissioners.

SEC. 6. That said Text-Book Commission shall hear and consider said report in its selection and adoption of a uniform series of text-books, and shall also, themselves, consider the merits of the books, taking into consideration their subject-matter, the printing, binding, material, and mechanical quality, and their general suitability and desirability for the purposes intended, and the price of said books, and they shall give due consideration to the report and recommendation of said sub-commission. Said Commission shall select and adopt such books as will, in their best judgment, accomplish the ends desired; and they are hereby authorized and directed, in case any book, or books are deemed by them suitable for adoption, and more desirable than other books, or book, of the same class, or division, submitted, and they further consider the price at which such book, or books, are offered to be unreasonably high, and that it should be offered at a smaller price, to immediately notify the publisher of such books, or book, of their decision, and request such reduction in price as

Text Book Commission, in selection of books, shall consider report of Sub-Commission and the books themselves.

Selection of books.

Procedure if price of book desired is unreasonably high.

they deem reasonable or just, and if they and such publishers shall agree on a price they may adopt this book, or books, but if not, they shall use their own sound judgment and discretion whether they will adopt that or the book, or books, deemed by them the next best in the list submitted. And when said Text-Book Commission shall have finished with the report of said sub-commission, the said report shall be filed and preserved in the office of the State Superintendent of Public Instruction, and shall be open at all times for public inspection.

<small>Discretion in adoption.</small>

<small>Report of Sub-Commission to be filed in office of Superintendent of Public Instruction.</small>

SEC. 7. That said Text-Book Commission shall, immediately after the passage of this act, meet and organize, the Governor being *ex officio* President of the Commission, and the Superintendent of Public Instruction its Secretary. As soon as practicable, not later than thirty days after its organization, the Commission shall advertise in such manner, and for such a length of time, and at such places as may be deemed advisable, that at a time and place fixed definitely in said advertisement sealed bids, or proposals, will be received from the publishers of school text-books for furnishing books to the public schools in the State of North Carolina, through agencies established by said publishers in several counties, and places in counties in the State, as may be provided for in such regulations as said Commission may adopt and prescribe. The bids, or proposals, to be for furnishing the books for a period of five years, and no longer, and that no bid for a longer period will be considered. Said bid, or bids, shall state specifically and definitely the price at which book, or books, are to be furnished, and shall be accompanied by ten or more specimen copies of each and every book proposed to be furnished, and it shall be required of each bidder to deposit with the Treasurer of the State a sum of money, such as the Commission may require, not less than $500, or more than $2,500, according to the number of books each bidder may propose to supply, and notice shall

<small>Organization of Commission.</small>

<small>Advertisement for bids for furnishing books.</small>

<small>Bids to be for furnishing books for five years.</small>

<small>Bid to state price, accompanied by specimen copies.</small>

<small>Bidder to deposit a sum of money with State Treasurer as pledge of good faith.</small>

further be given in said advertisement that such deposits shall be forfeited absolutely to the State if the bidder making the deposit of any sum shall fail, or refuse, to make and execute such contract and bond, as is hereinafter required, within such time as the Commission shall require, which time shall also be stated in said advertisement. All bids shall be sealed and deposited with the Secretary of State, to be by him delivered to the Commission when they are in executive session, for the purpose of considering the same, when they shall be opened in the presence of the Commission.

SEC. 8. That it shall be the duty of the said Text-Book Commission to meet at the time and place designated in such notice, or advertisement, and take out the sample, or specimen, copies submitted, upon which the bids are based, and refer and submit them to the sub-commission, as provided for and directed in section 3 of this act, with instructions to the said sub-commission to report back to them, at a time specified, with their report, classification, and recommendation, as provided in sections 3 and 4. When the said report is submitted it shall be the duty of the said Text-Book Commission to meet in executive session to open and examine all sealed proposals submitted and received in pursuance of the notice, or advertisement, provided for in section 7 of this act. It shall be the duty of said Commission to examine and consider carefully all such bids, or proposals, together with the report and recommendation of the sub-commission, and determine in the manner provided in section 6 of this act what book, or books, upon the branch hereinabove mentioned, shall be selected for adoption, taking into consideration the size, quality as to the subject-matter, material, printing, binding, and the mechanical execution, and price, and the general suitability for the purpose desired and intended: *Provided, however,* that all books selected, or adopted, shall be written, or printed, in English. After their selection, or adoption, shall have been made, the said Commission shall, by registered letter, notify the publishers, or proposers, to whom the contracts have been awarded, and it shall be the duty of the Attorney-General of the State to prepare the said contract, or contracts, in accordance with the terms, or provisions, of this act, and the said contract shall be executed by the Governor and the Secretary of State, and the seal of the State attached upon the part of the State of North Carolina, and the said contract shall be executed in triplicate, one copy to be kept by the contractor, one copy to be kept by the Secretary of the Text-Book Commission, and one copy to be filed in the office of the Secretary of State. At the time of the execution of the contract aforesaid, the contractor shall enter into a bond in the sum of not less than ten thousand dollars, payable to the State of North Carolina, the amount of said bond, within said limits, to be fixed by said Commission, conditioned for the faithful, honest, and exact performance of this contract, and shall further provide for the payment of reasonable attorney's fees in case of recovery in any suit upon the same, with three or more good and solvent sureties, actual citizens and residents of the State of North Carolina, or any guaranty company authorized to do business in the State of North Carolina, may become the surety on the said bond; and it shall be the duty of the Attorney-General to prepare and approve said bond: *Provided, however*, that said bond shall not be exhausted by a single recovery, but may be sued on from time to time until the full amount thereof shall be recovered, and the said Commission may, at any time, by giving thirty days' notice, require additional security or additional bond. And when any firm, person, or corporation shall have been awarded a contract, and submitted therewith the bond as required hereunder, the Commission, through its Secretary, shall so inform the Treasurer of the State, and it shall then be the duty of the Treasurer to return to such contractor the cash deposit made by him, and the said Commission, through its Secretary, shall inform the Treasurer of the names of such unsuccessful bidders, or proposers, and the Treasurer shall, upon the receipt of this notice, return to them the amount deposited by them in cash at the time of the submission of their bids. But should any person, firm, or company, or corporation fail, or refuse, to execute a contract, and submit therewith his bond as required by this act, within thirty days of the awarding of the contract to him, and the mailing of the registered letter containing the notice: *Provided,* the mailing of the registered letter shall be sufficient evidence that the notice was given and received, the said cash deposit shall be deemed and is hereby declared forfeited to the State of North Carolina and it shall be the duty of the Treasurer to place such cash deposit in the Treasury of the State to the credit of the school fund; *And provided further,* that any recovery had on any bond given by any contractor shall inure to the benefit of the school fund in the State and counties, and when collected shall be placed in the Treasury of the school fund.

SEC. 9. That the books furnished under any contract shall, at all times during the existence of the contract be equal to, in all respects, the specimen, or sample, copies furnished with the bid, and it shall be the duty of the Secretary of State to carefully preserve in his office, as the standard of quality and excellence to be maintained in such books during the continuance of such contracts, the specimen, or sample, copies of all books which have been the basis of any contract, together with the original bid, or proposal. It shall be the duty of all contractors to print plainly on the back of each book the contract price, as well as the exchange price at which it is agreed to be furnished, but the books submitted as sample, or specimen copies, with the original bid shall not have the price printed on them before they are submitted to the sub-commission. And the said Text-Book Commission shall not, in any case, contract with any person, publisher, or publishers, for the use of any book, or books, which are to be, or shall be, sold to patrons for use in any public school in the State, at above, or in excess of, the price at which such book, or books, are furnished by said person, publisher, or publishers, under contract to any State, county, or school district in the United States, under like conditions as those prevailing in this State and under this act. And it shall be stipulated in each contract that the contractor has never furnished, and is not now furnishing, under contract, any State, county or school district in the United States, where like conditions prevail as are prevailing in this State, and under this act, the same book, or books, as are embraced in said contract at a price below or less than price stipulated in said contract, and the said Commission is hereby authorized and directed, at any time that they may find that any book, or books, have been sold at a lower price under contract to any State, county, or school district aforesaid, to sue upon the bond of said contractor and recover the difference between the contract and the lower price for which they find the book, or books, have been sold. And in case any contractor shall fail to execute specifically the terms and provisions of his contract, said Commission is hereby authorized, empowered, and directed to bring suit upon the bond of such contractor for the recovery of any and all damages, the suit to be in the name of the State of North Carolina, and the recovery for the benefit of the public school fund. But nothing in this act shall be construed so as to prevent said Commission and any contractor agreeing thereto from in any manner changing or altering any contract: *Provided,* four members of the Commission shall agree to the change, and think it advisable and for the best interest of the public schools of this State.

48

State not liable to contractor.

SEC. 10. That it shall always be a part of the terms and conditions of every contract made in pursuance of this act, that the State of North Carolina shall not be liable to any contractor in any manner for any sum whatever, but all such contractors shall receive their pay, or **Compensation of contractor, solely from proceeds of book sales.** consideration, in compensation solely and exclusively derived from the proceeds of the sale of books as provided for in this act:

Contractors to take old books in exchange for new at not less than fifty per cent of contract price.

Provided further, that the Commission shall stipulate in the contract for the supplying of any book, or books, as herein provided, that the contractor, or contractors, shall take up school books now in use in this State and receive the same in exchange of new books, allowing a price for such old books not less than fifty per cent of the contract price of the new books. And each person or publisher, mak-**Bids to state exchange price of books furnished.** a bid for the supplying of any book, or books, hereunder, shall state in such bid, or proposal, the exchange price at which such book, or books, shall be furnished.

Right to reject bids reserved.

SEC. 11. That the Text-Book Commission shall have and reserve the right to reject any and all bids, or proposals, if they shall be of opinion that any or all should, for **Failure to adopt from bids submitted, Commission may re-advertise.** any reason, be rejected. And in case they fail from among the bids, or proposals submitted, to select, or adopt, any book, or books, from any of the branches mentioned in section 2 of this act, they may re-advertise for sealed bids, **Same provisions to apply.** or proposals, under the same terms and conditions as before, and proceed in their investigations in all respects as they did in the first instance, and as required by the **May advertise for bids for books in manuscript, not published** terms and provisions of this act, or they may advertise for sealed bids, or proposals, from authors, or publishers, of text-books, who have manuscripts of books not yet published, for prices at which they will publish and furnish in book form such manuscripts for use in the public schools in North Carolina, proceeding in like manner as **State can not contract to pay for publication.** before; *And Provided further,* the State itself shall not, under any circumstances, enter into any contract binding it to pay for the publication of any book, or books, but in the contract with the owner of the manuscript it shall be provided that he shall pay the compensation to the publisher for the publication and putting in book form the manuscript, together with the cost and expenses of copyrighting the same; *And Provided further,* that in all cases bids, or proposals, shall be accompanied with a cash deposit of from $500 to $2,500, as the Commission may direct, and as provided in section 7 of this act. And it is further expressly provided, that any person, firm, or corporation, now doing business, or proposing to do business, in the State of North Carolina, shall have the right to bid for the contract to be awarded hereunder in manner as follows: In response to the advertisement, when made as hereinbefore provided, said person, firms, or corporations, may submit the written bid, or bids, to edit, or have edited, published and supplied for use in the public schools in this State any book, or books, provided for hereunder: *Provided,* that instead of filing with the said bids, or proposals, a sample or specimen, of copy of each book proposed to be furnished, he may exhibit to the Commission in manuscript, or printed form, the matter proposed to be incorporated in any book, together with such a description and illustration of the form and style thereof, as will be fully intelligible and satisfactory to the said Commission, or he may submit a book, or books, the equal of which in every way they propose to furnish; and he shall accompany his bids, or proposals, with cash deposit hereinbefore provided:

Provided, that all books and manuscripts shall be examined and reported upon by said sub-commission provided for in section 3 of this act.

Sec. 12. That as soon as said Commission shall have entered into a contract, or contracts, for the furnishing, or supplying, of books for use in the public schools in this State, it shall be the duty of the Governor to issue his proclamation announcing such fact to the people of the State.

Sec. 13. That there shall be maintained in each county in the State, provided the Commission shall deem it advisable, and so demand, not less than one, or more than six, agencies for the distribution of the books to the patrons, or the contractor shall be permitted to make arrangements with merchants, or others, for the handling and distribution of the books, and parties living in the county where no agency has been established, or no arrangement made for distribution, may order the same from one of the contractors, and it shall be the duty of the contractor, or contractors, to deliver any book, or books, so ordered, to the person ordering, to his post-office address, freight, express, postage, or other charges, prepaid, at the retail contract price: *Provided,* the price of the book, or books, so ordered shall be paid in advance. All books shall be sold to the consumer at the retail contract price, and on each book shall be printed the following: "The price fixed hereon is fixed by State contract, and any deviation therefrom shall be reported to your County Superintendent of Public Instruction, or the State Superintendent at Raleigh." And it is expressly provided that should any party contracting to furnish books, as provided for in this act, fail to furnish them, or otherwise breach his contract, in addition to the right of the State to sue on the bond hereinabove required, the chairman of the County Board of Education, or any member of said Board of Education, may sue in the name of the State of North Carolina, in the courts of the State of North Carolina having jurisdiction, and recover on the bond given by the contractor the full value of the books so failed to be furnished, for the use and benefit of the school fund of the county: *Provided,* that in all cases service of process may be had and deemed sufficient on any agent of the contractor in the county, or if no agent is in the county, then service of any depository, and this service shall be, and stand in the place of service on the defendant contractor.

SEC. 14. That said Commission may, from time to time, make any necessary regulations not contrary to the provisions of this act, to secure the prompt distribution of the books herein provided for, and the prompt and faithful performance of all contracts, and it is especially now provided that said Commission shall maintain its organization during the five years of the continuance of the contract, and after the expiration of the same to re-advertise for new bids, or proposals, as required by this act, in the first instance, and enter into such other contracts as they may deem best for the interest of the patrons of the public schools of the State: *Provided,* any contract entered into, or renewed, shall be for the term of five years. {Power of Commission to make regulations. Term of Commission. At expiration of five years Commission to re-advertise and contract. Renewed contract to be for five years.}

SEC. 15. That as soon as practicable after the adoption provided for in this act, the State Superintendent shall issue a circular letter to each County Superintendent in the State, and to such others as he may desire to send it, which letter shall contain the list of books adopted, the prices, location of agencies, and method of distribution, and such other information as he may deem necessary. {Immediately after adoption, State Superintendent to notify County Superintendents.}

SEC. 16. That as soon after the passage of this act as may be practicable, and the Commission shall deem advisable, the books adopted as a uniform system of text-books shall be introduced and used as text-books, to the exclusion of all others in all the public free schools in the State: *Provided,* that nothing herein shall be so construed as to prevent the use of supplementary books, but such supplementary books shall not be used to the exclusion of the books prescribed, or adopted, under the provisions of this act: *And provided, further,* that nothing in this act shall prevent the teaching in any school any branch higher, or more advanced, than is embraced in section 2 of this act, nor the use of any book upon such higher branch of study: *Provided,* that such higher {Books adopted to be exclusively used in public schools as soon as practicable. Proviso as to supplementary books. Proviso as to teaching higher branches and use of books therein.}

branch shall not be taught to the exclusion of the branches mentioned and set out in section 2 of this act.

If no contract made, or contractor fails to furnish books, patrons may procure in usual way.

SEC. 17. That nothing herein shall be construed to prevent or prohibit the patrons of the public schools throughout the State from procuring books in the usual way, in case no contract shall be made, or the contractor fails, or refuses, to furnish the books provided for in this act at the time required for their use in the respective schools.

Penalty for teacher wilfully using or permitting to be used books other than those adopted upon the same branch.

SEC. 18. That any teacher who shall wilfully use, or permit to be used, in his or her school, any text-book upon the branches embraced in this act, where the Commission has adopted a book upon that branch, other than the one so adopted, the County Board of Education shall discharge and cancel the certificate of said teacher, or school superintendent: *Provided,* that they may use, or permit to be used, such book, or books, as may now be owned by the pupils of the school, until such books are worn out, not exceeding one year from date of adoption.

How long books now in use may be used.

Penalty for selling books for a greater than contract price.

SEC. 19. That any dealer, clerk, or agent, who shall sell any book for a greater price than the contract price shall be guilty of a misdemeanor, and upon conviction shall be punished by a fine not exceeding $50.00.

Text-Book Commission to serve without compensation.
Compensation of Sub-Commission.

SEC. 20. That said Text-Book Commission shall serve without compensation, and members of the sub-commission actually serving shall be paid a per diem of four dollars per day, during the time that they are actually engaged, not to exceed thirty days, and in addition shall be repaid all money actually expended by them in the payment of necessary expenses, to be paid out of the public school fund, and they shall make out and swear to an itemized statement of such expenses.

Must make verified expense account.

Conflicting laws repealed.

SEC. 21. That all laws and clauses of laws in conflict with this act be and the same are hereby repealed.

SEC. 22. That this act shall be in force from and after its ratification.

In the General Assembly read three times, and ratified this the 8th day of February, A. D. 1901.

INDEX TO SCHOOL LAW.

A

	SECTION.
Action on Sheriffs' bonds, how brought	54
Additional powers of Boards of Education	14
Amount of contracts restricted	34
Annual report of State Superintendent	5
Annual settlement of school business, second Monday of July	59
Appeals can be taken from decisions of County Boards to condemn land	31
Appeals from decisions of County Boards affecting one's character or right to teach	15
Apportionment made on basis of population	1
Apportionment of school funds	24
Apportionment semi-annual	25
Appropriations for Teachers' Institutes	26
Auditor to send out revised forms of blanks for tax lists	60
Auditor to keep separate accounts of school funds	1

B

Branches taught in public schools	37
Boundaries of school districts	20

C

County Board of Education—To estimate amount necessary to maintain schools for four months	6
How elected	12
When to enter upon duties	12
How to fill vacancies	12
Term of office	12
Corporate body	13
Duties and powers	13
To obey instructions of State Superintendent and his constructions of school law	13
To fix time for opening and closing public schools	13
To make needful rules and regulations for conducting schools	13
Powers over teachers and applicants	15
Chairman to report election of County Superintendent to State Superintendent	16
To appoint School Committeemen	17
Compensation of County Boards	27
Time of regular meetings	27
To examine books, vouchers and accounts of Treasurer	27
Power to punish for contempt	28
Power to receive gifts, dispose of property, deeds, proceeds	30
May receive suitable sites by donation or purchase	31
Power to condemn sites and report to Clerk of Superior Court	31
To provide office for County Superintendent	36
Authority to remove County Superintendent on complaint of State Superintendent for immorality or neglect of duty	10

	SECTION.
County Board of Education—*Continued*.	
Authority to remove County Superintendent on complaint of State Superintendent for failure to make report	11
To apportion the school fund	24
To make appropriation for Teachers' Institutes	26
To divide townships into school districts	29
To form a school district out of portions of contiguous townships	29
To administer oaths	16
To take oath to perform duties	45
To fix maximum salary of teachers	24
Committeemen—How appointed	17
Compensation to Township Committeemen	17
To furnish school census report	20
Compensation for making census	20
To organize and record proceedings, etc.	18
To care for school property	19
To keep permanent record of expenditures, etc.	21 to 35
Power to employ and dismiss teachers	22
To give order for teachers' salaries	23
Power to close schools	23
May contract with principal of private school	33
To give notice of election of teachers	20
County Superintendent—How and when elected	16
Qualifications	16
Term of office	16
Furnish blanks for committeemen	20
Authority over teachers of private schools where public fund is used	33
To administer oaths	16
To take oath to perform duties	45
Secretary Board of Education	36
To issue notices and orders of County Board	36
To record school statistics	36
To look after forfeitures, fines and penalties	36
To examine teachers	37
Shall not renew second-grade certificate except upon re-examination	37
To hold teachers' meeting in each township	38
To advise with teachers	39
Power to suspend teachers with concurrence of School Committee.	39
Required to visit schools	39
To distribute school registers, blanks for statistics, and to have statistics fully and properly reported	40
To make annual report to State Superintendent on or before July 1st	41
To keep a copy of report to State Superintendent	41
To furnish list of dumb and blind children	43
Compensation	44
Residence	44
Unlawful to teach school	44
To sign vouchers, orders, etc	48
County Commissioners—To approve Treasurers' bond	47
To order special school tax elections	72
To bring action against defaulting Sheriff	54
Commissioners of incorporated towns authorized to order elections for schools	71

SECTION.

Clerks of Court—To furnish County Boards statement of fines, forfeitures, etc. 62
   To record and keep deeds 32
Certificates, grades, etc. 37

D

Deeds. (See Clerk of Court.)
Districts, how formed, etc. 29
Duties of teachers in schools 63
Dismissal of pupils 63

E

Examination of teachers—Where, when conducted, fees, etc. 37
   Employment of teachers 20

F

Fiscal school year 67
Formation of districts from contiguous townships 29
Funds, how and where expended 6
Funds, how apportioned to equalize school terms 24

G

Grades. (See certificates.) 37

I

Institutes, by whom conducted 26

M

Misdemeanor for County Treasurer to fail to do any duty required 53
Misdemeanor to disturb school or injure school property 28
Minimum distance between schools 29
Minimum number of children to school district 29

O

Oaths—Members of County Boards, Committeemen and Superintendents to take oath to perform duties 45
Orders—For teachers' salaries, limit to amount of order 48
   For building and repairs not to be paid till title passed 48
   On Treasurer, when valid 23

P

Pay students 65
Proceeds from swamp lands, grants, etc., to be appropriated to public schools 4
Proceeds from estrays, fines, penalties, forfeitures, liquor licenses to remain in counties for school fund 5
Power to employ and dismiss teachers 22
Place for holding examination 37
Qualifications of County Superintendent. (See County Superintendent.)

R

Right of Superior Courts to review actions of County Boards 15
Report of number of public school-houses and value 20
Report of list of persons unable to read and write 20
Restrictions as to third grade certificates 22
Restrictions on Committee in giving orders 34
Restrictions on use of annual school fund 34
Restrictions in purchase of school supplies 69
Removal of School Committeemen 42

	SECTION.
Register of Deeds to furnish County Boards abstract of tax lists	61
Report of teachers to County Superintendent	64
Right of children to attend school, section 1810 of Code	68

S

State Board of Education, duties and powers	1, 2, 16, 44, 70
State Superintendent of Public Instruction, duties and powers.	7, 8, 9, 10, 11, 26
Special school tax, how levied	71
School, public, defined	65
School funds paid into treasury, how held and paid out	3
School month defined	22
School year defined	67
School term to be continuous	22
School district, how formed	29
Sheriffs to serve subpœnas	15
Sheriffs to settle with County Treasurer on or before December 1st of each year	51
Sheriffs to take duplicate receipts, to transmit one copy to State Auditor, the other to chairman of County Board of Education	55
Sheriffs to give itemized receipts according to section 51	56
State Board of Examiners—How and when appointed, powers and duties, meetings and compensation	70
Solicitors—Duties as to penalties, etc.	5

T

Tax—On what levied, and how collected	6
Teachers—How employed	20
To exhibit statement to committee	23
Required to attend Institutes	26
To pay fee for private examination	37
To keep daily record	64
To file record at end of school	64
Duties in school	63
To make monthly statements	23
To be examined second Thursday in July and October	37
Text-Book Law appended.	
Treasurer—To be notified of apportionment	24
To receive and disburse county school funds	46
To execute bond, liable for funds illegally paid	48
To keep books showing amount apportioned each township and district; to balance accounts annually	49
To produce books, vouchers and exhibit school moneys	50
To report to State Superintendent first Monday in August entire amount of money received and disbursed by him for schools and file duplicate with County Board	51
To receive money only from Sheriff or collecting officer	52
To be guilty of misdemeanor for failure to perform any duty required in this act	53
To file report when term of office expires	57
To deposit books, blanks, etc., in office of County Board	58
To attend his office last Saturday of each month to pay school claims: compensation	58

V

Vouchers, when valid	48

W

When committee may order school closed	23

CPSIA information can be obtained
at www.ICGtesting.com
Printed in the USA
LVHW020102250323
742526LV00012B/602